Get FREE Mandalas Every Month!
Join Our FREE Monthly Mandala Club at:
http://Club.ColoringForGrownUps.net

Introduction:

Thanks for purchasing Pocket Mandala 2 by Charles Orlik. We know you will find this collection of Mandalas a hit for fun on the go. Perfect to pop into your purse or briefcase you can now take coloring fun on the train ride to work, at lunchtime, while you are on a trip, etc. The possibilities are endless.

Are you enjoying this book? Please rate and review on Amazon. I highly appreciate it.

Please keep in touch:
Facebook: https://www.facebook.com/newadultcoloringbooks
Twitter: @coloring_books1

To see my other releases, visit my Amazon Store link:
Web: www.ColoringForGrownUps.Net

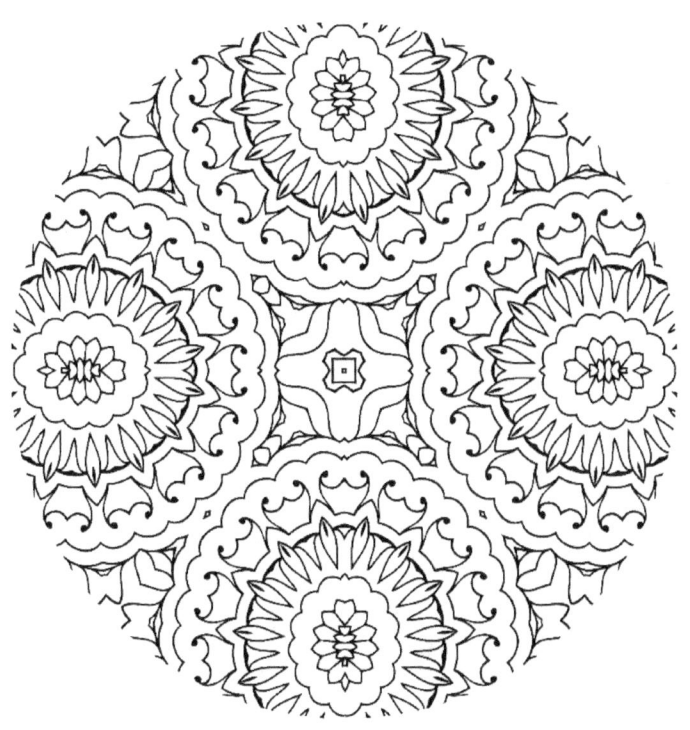

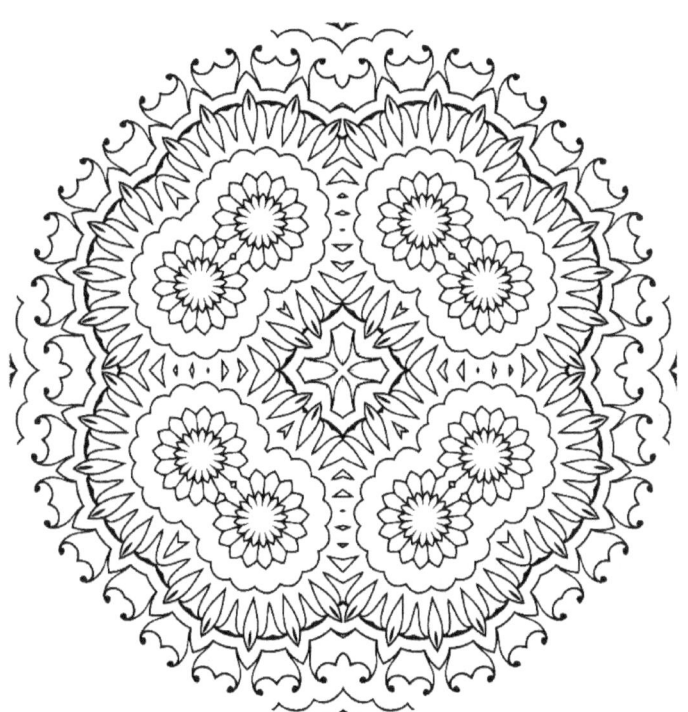

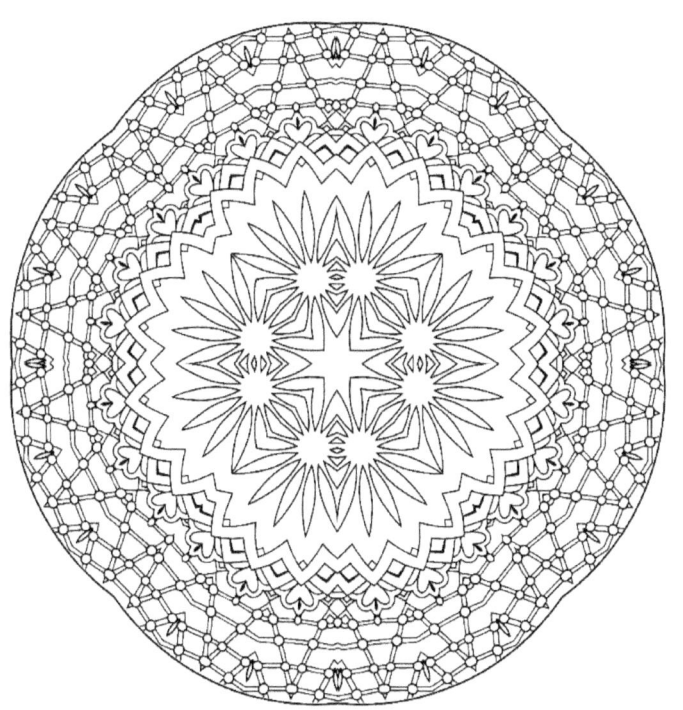

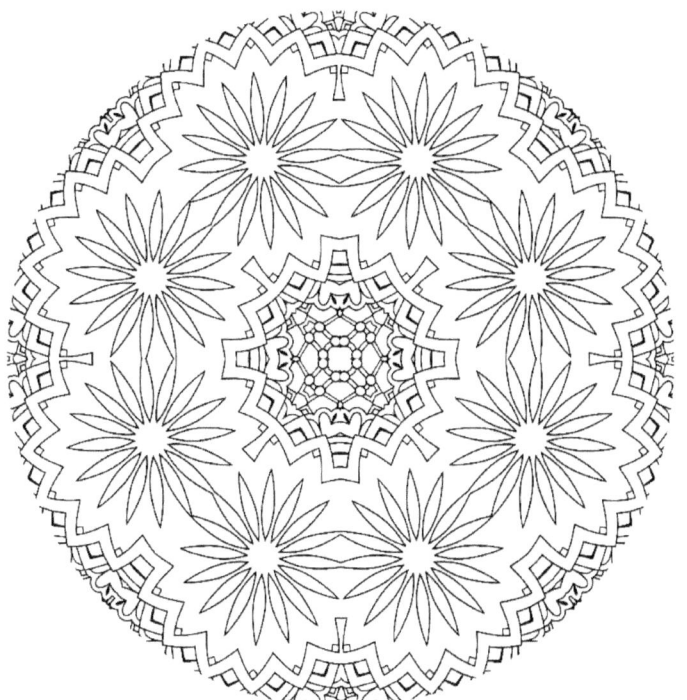

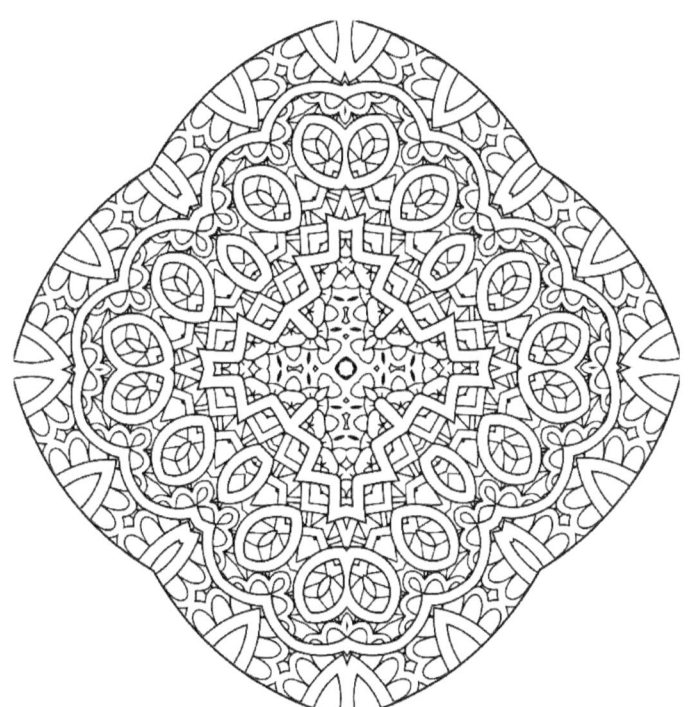

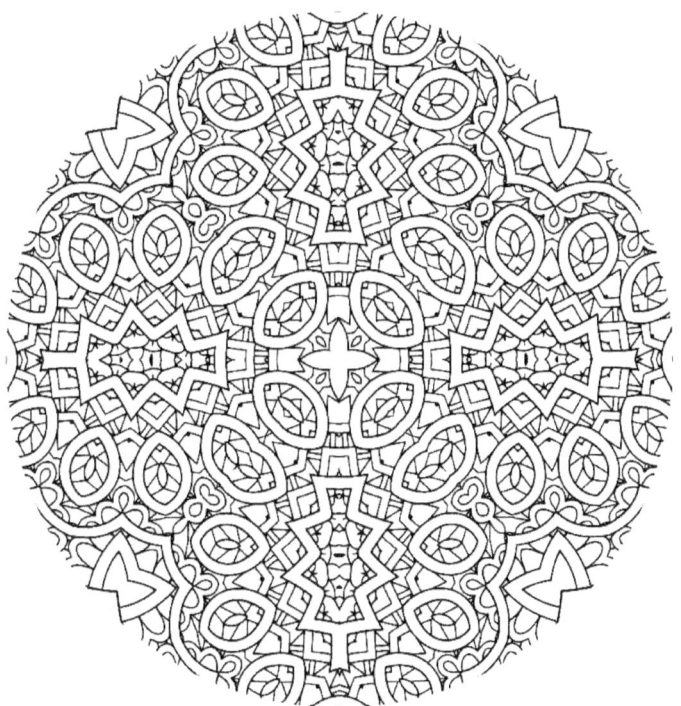

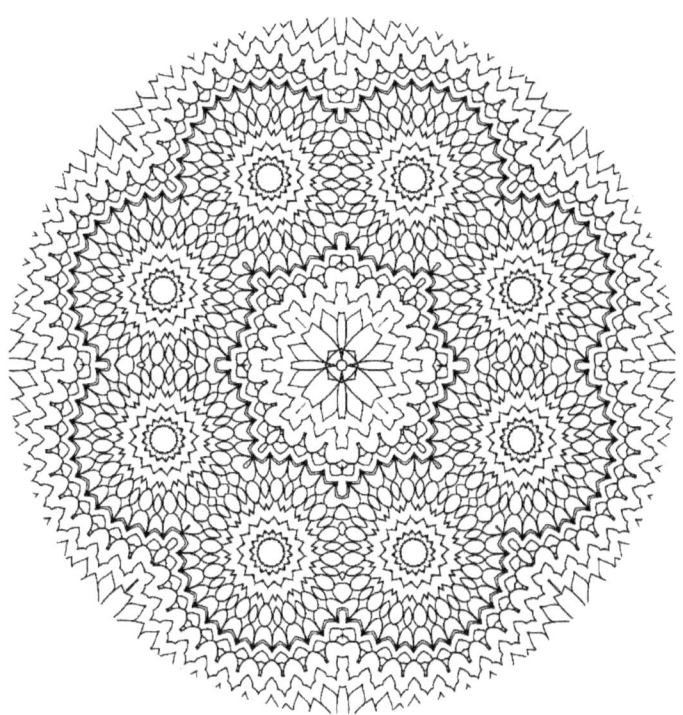

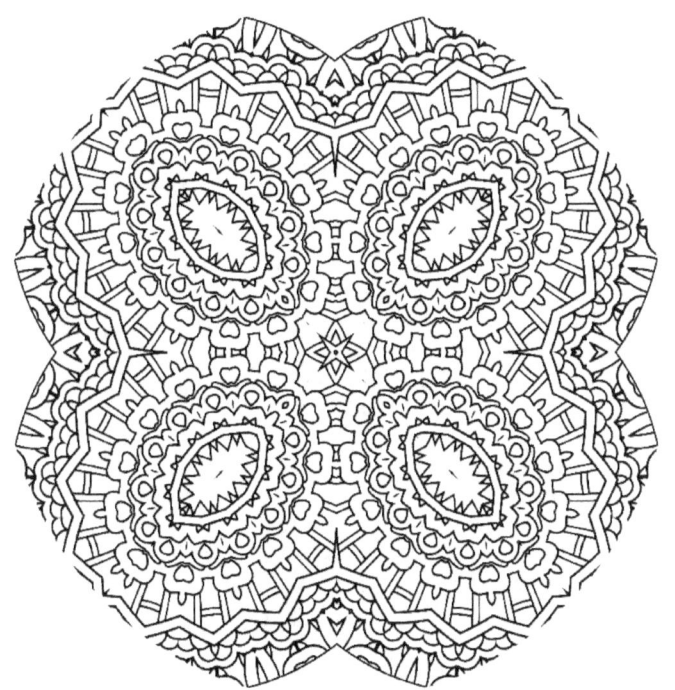

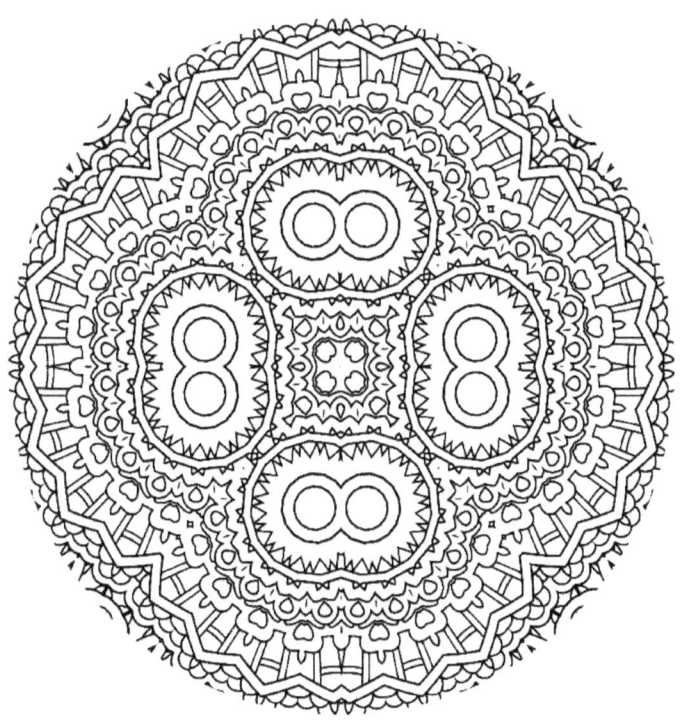

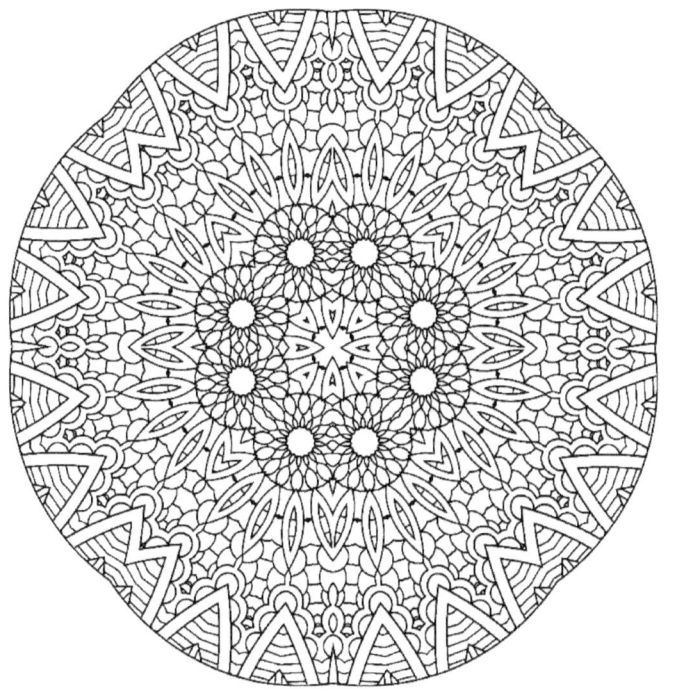

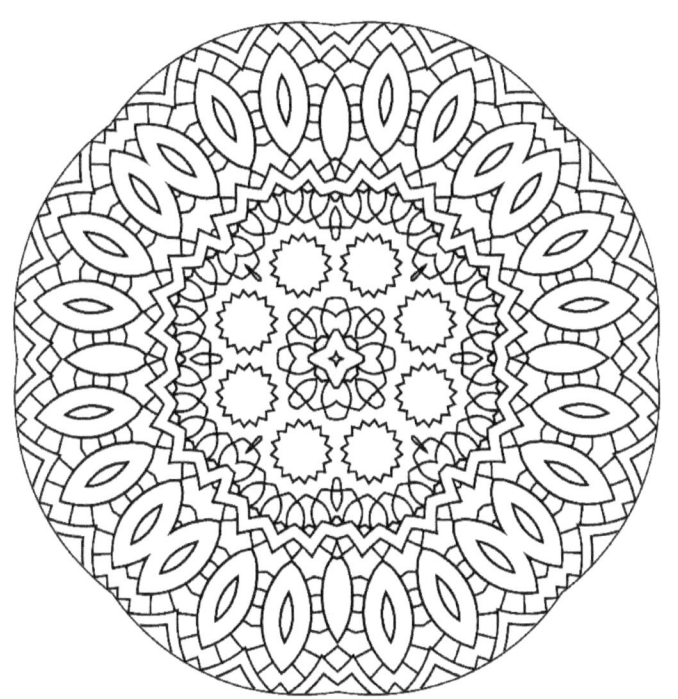

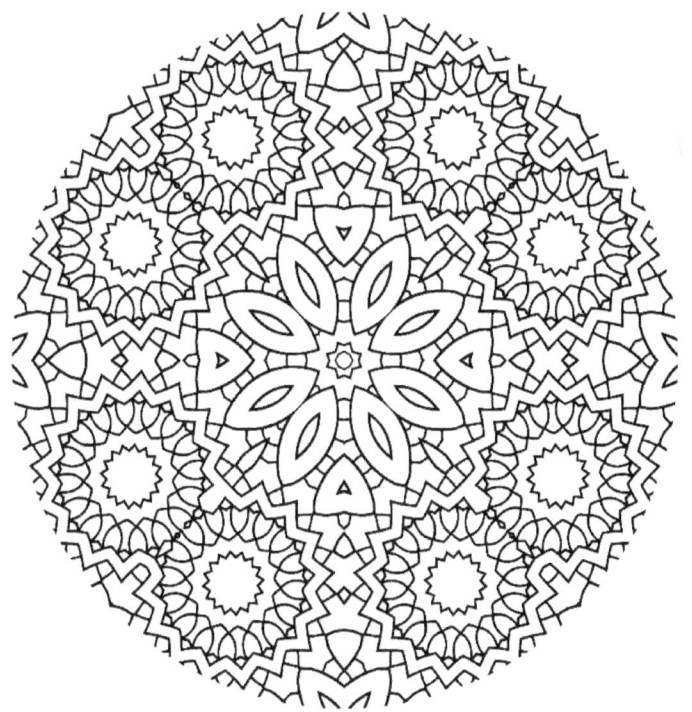

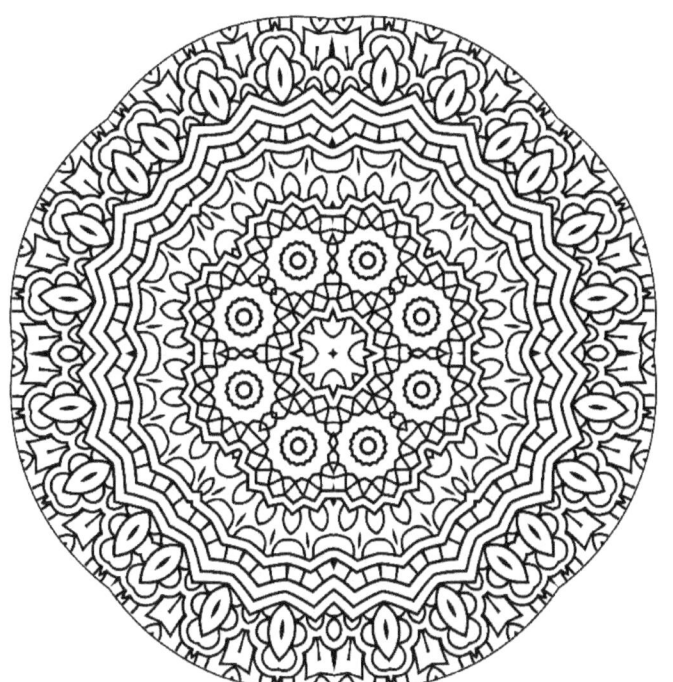

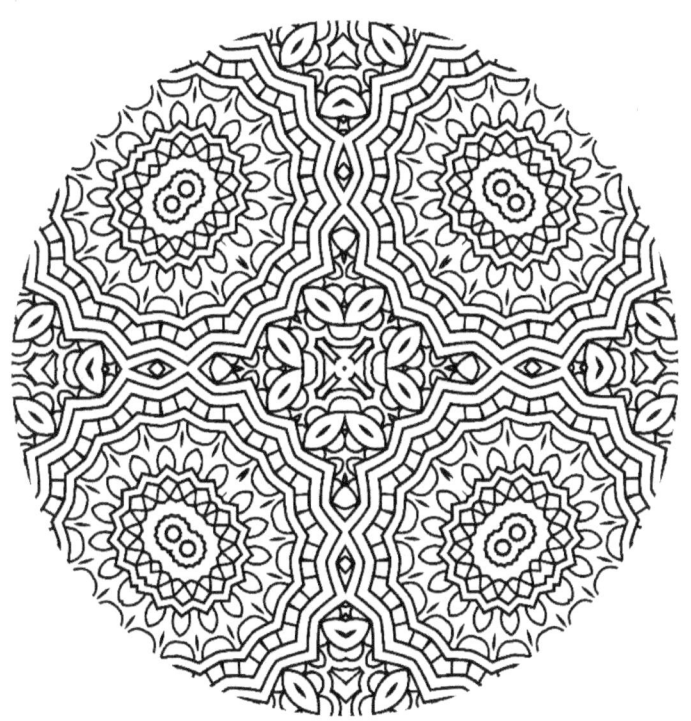

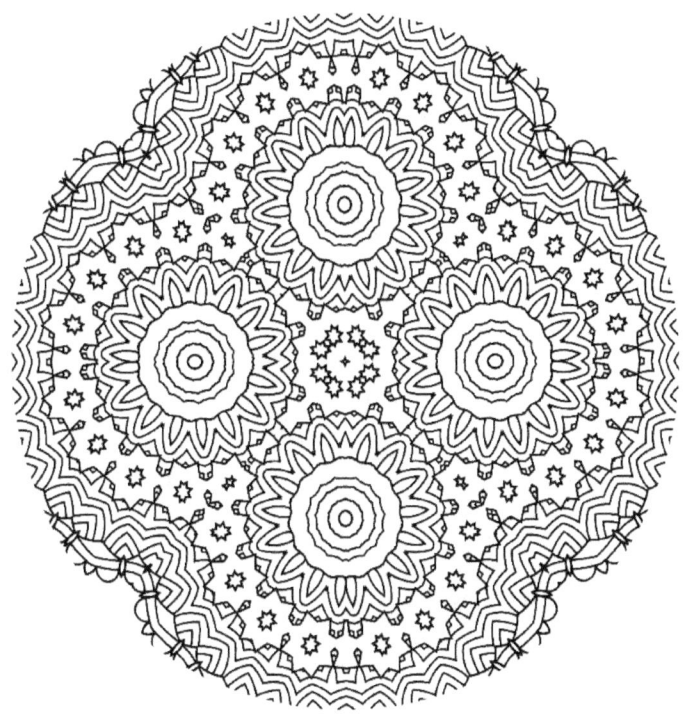

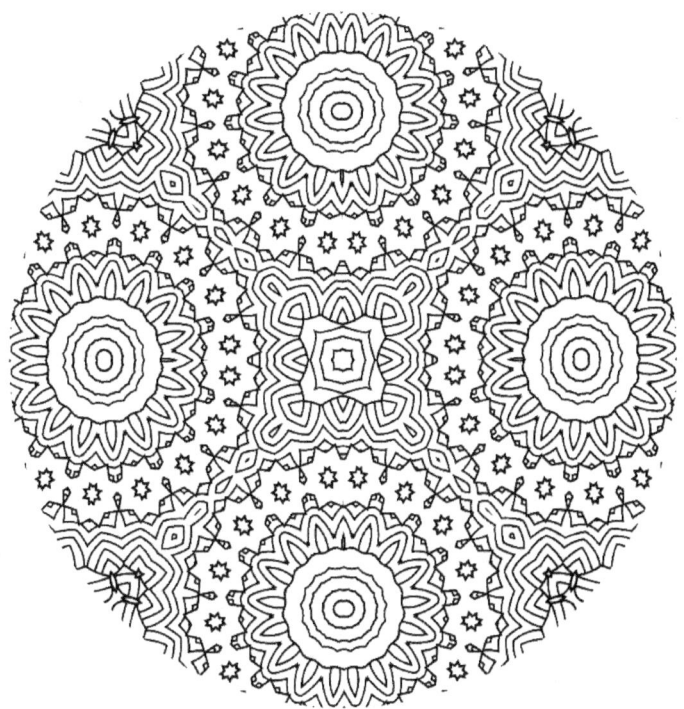

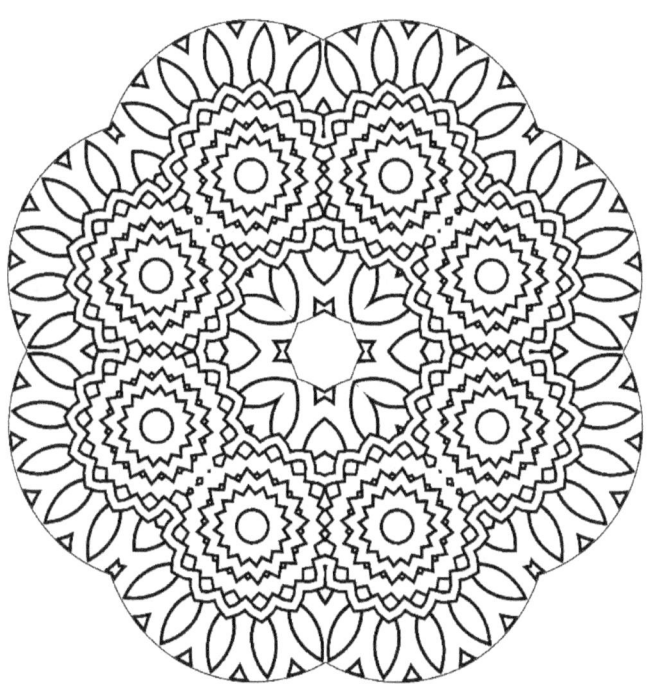

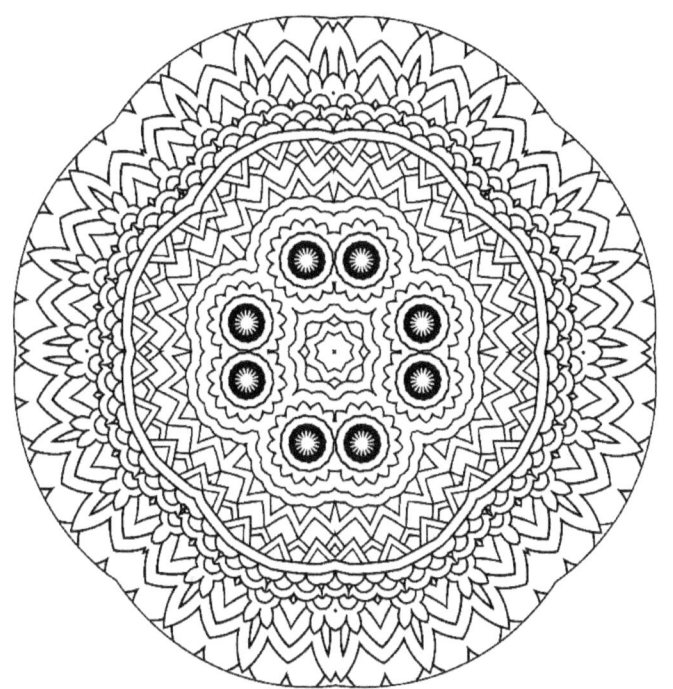

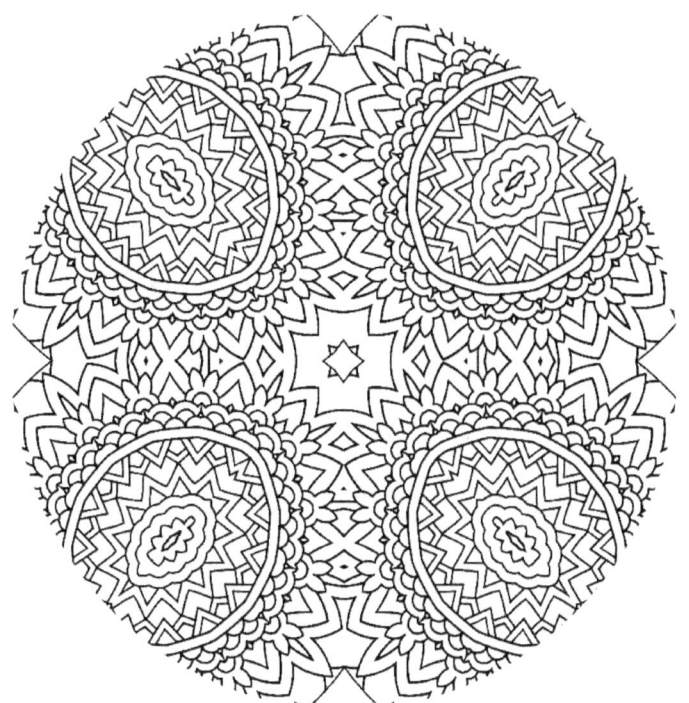

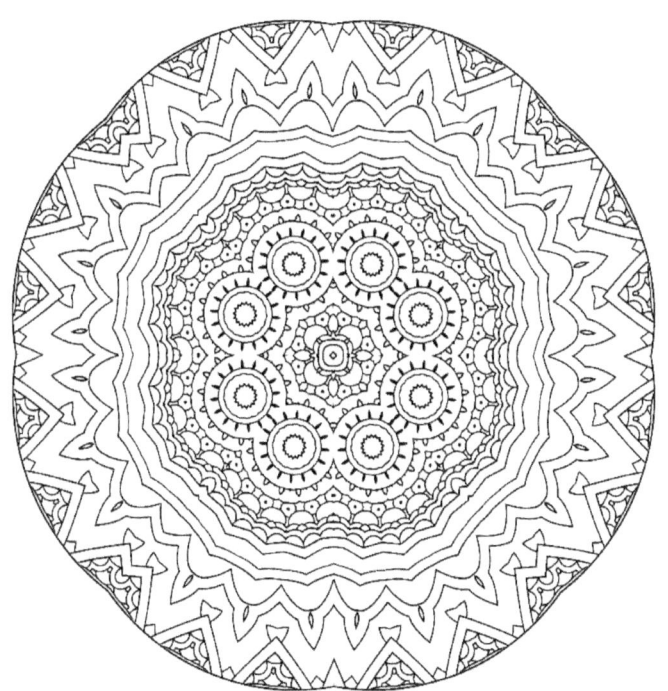

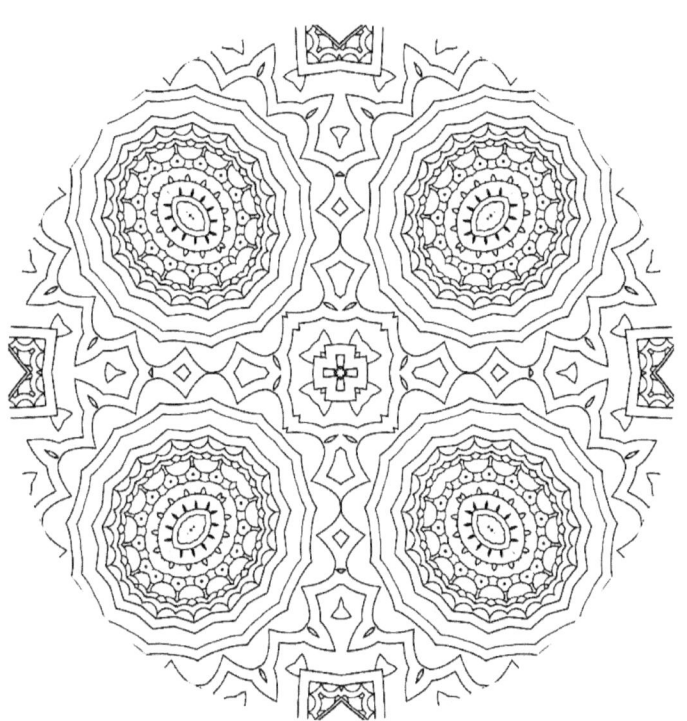

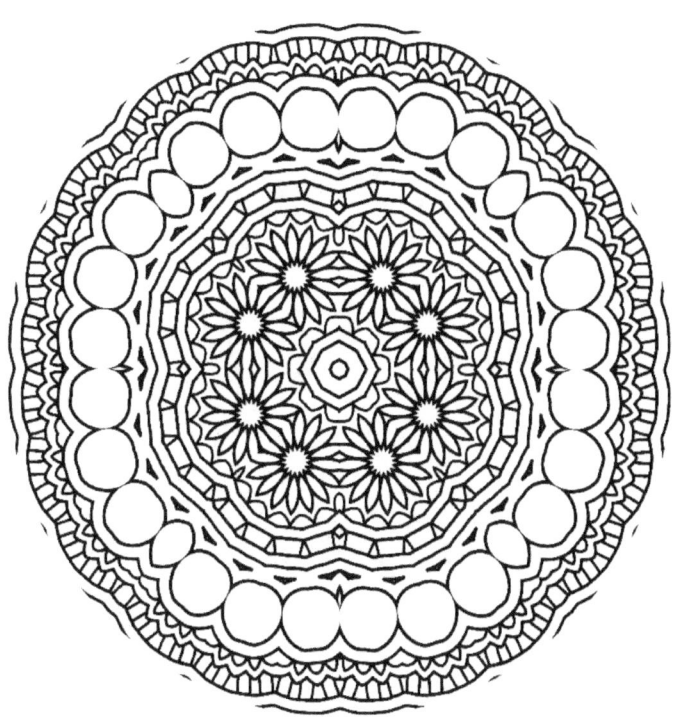

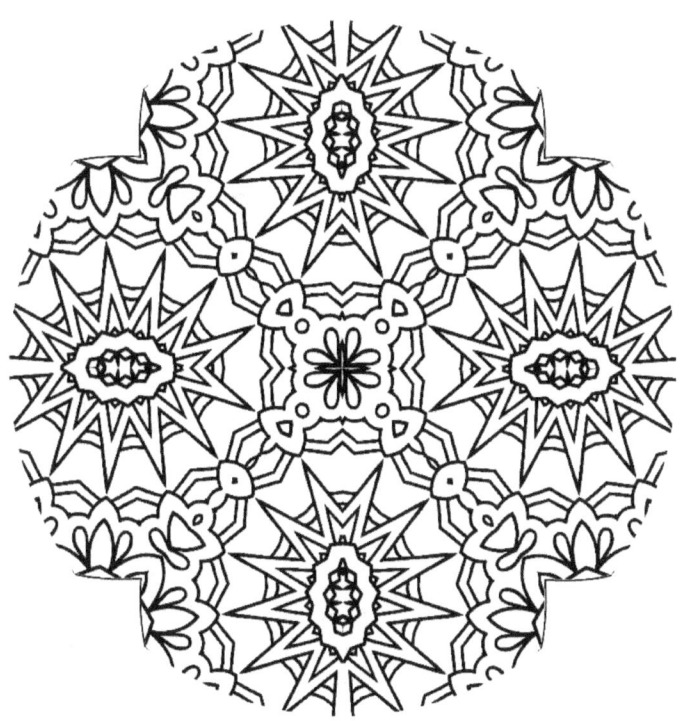

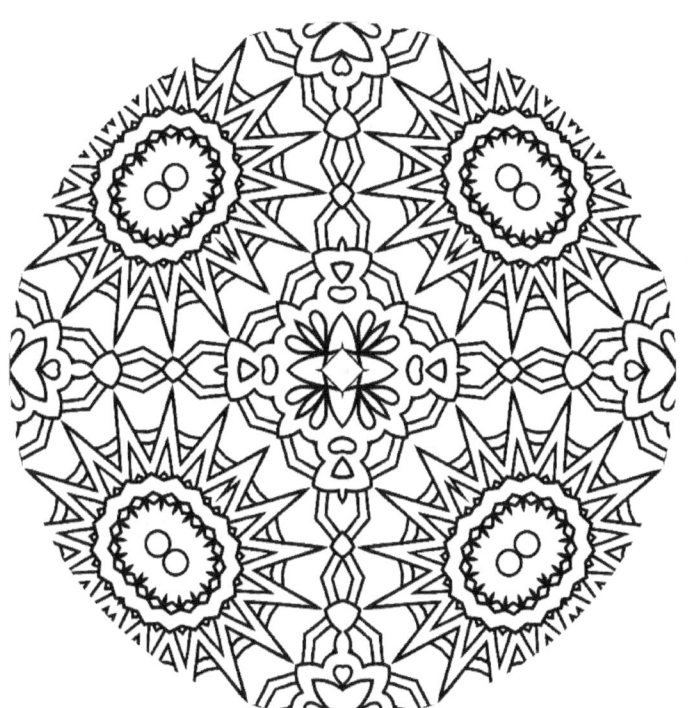

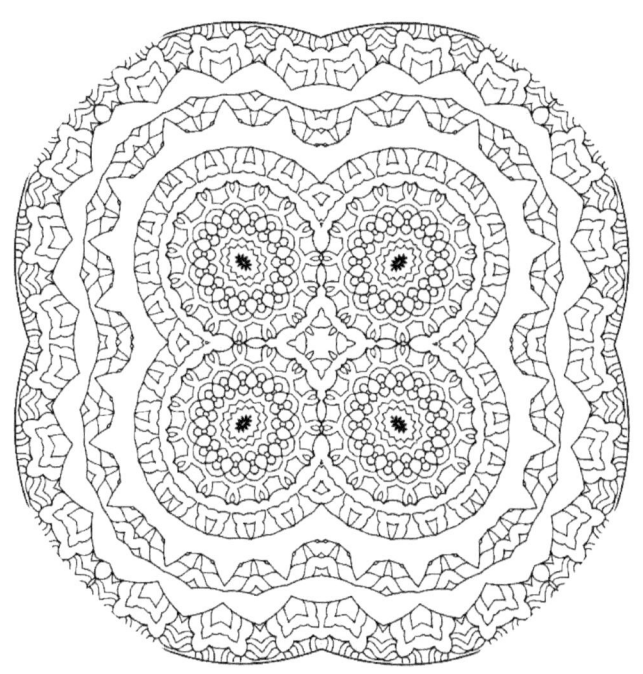

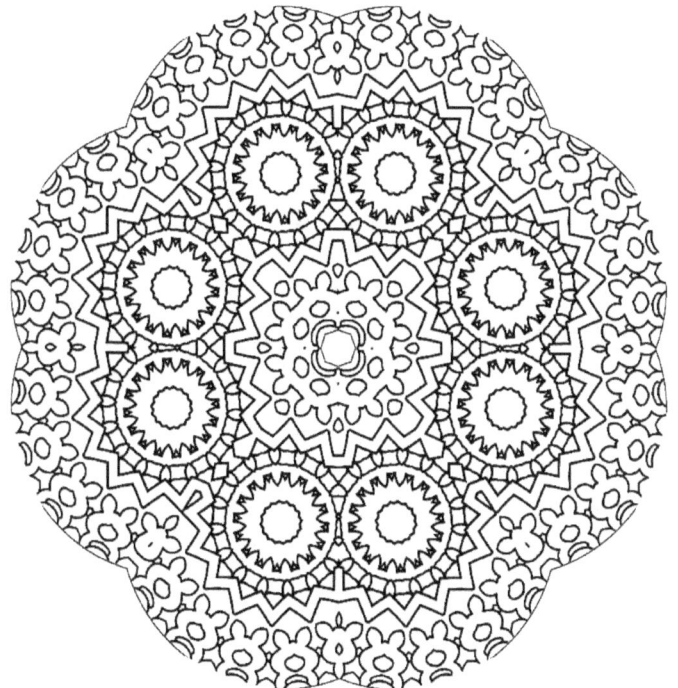

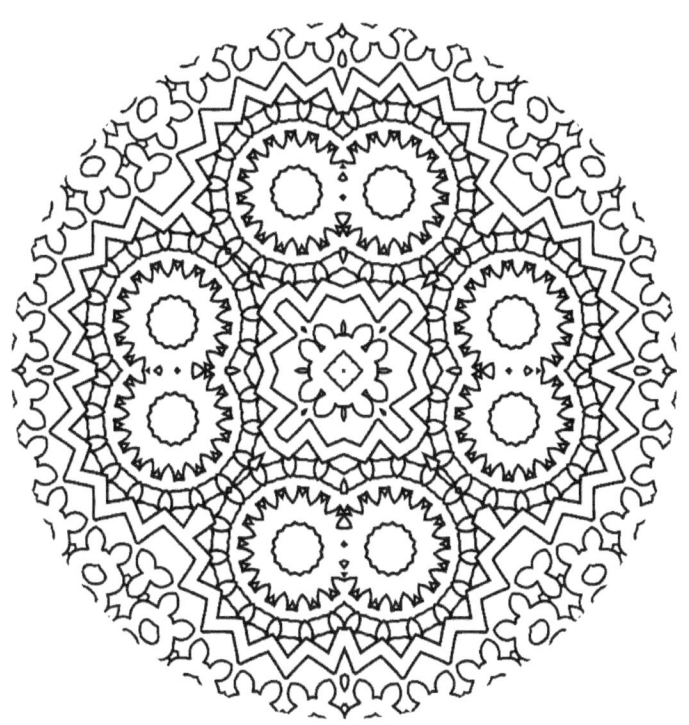

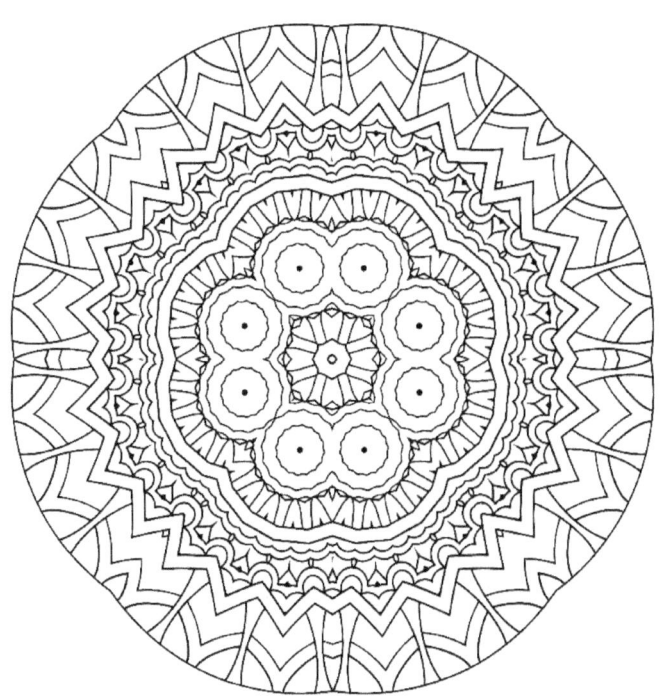

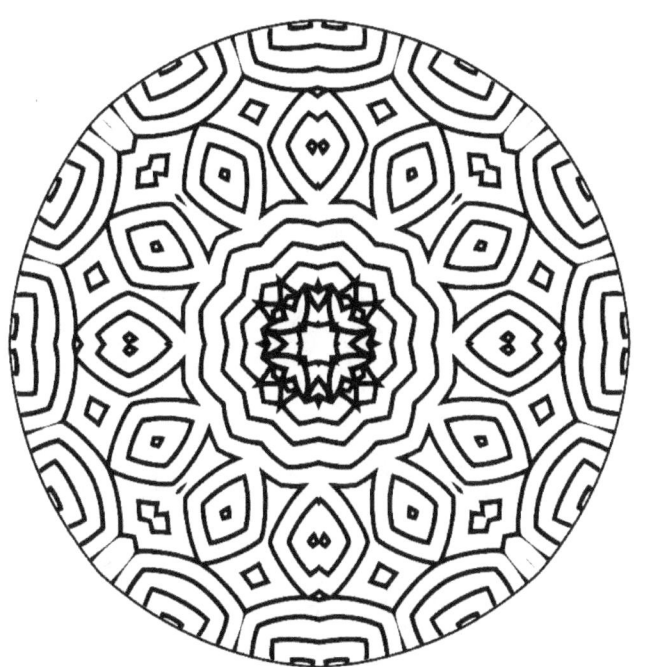

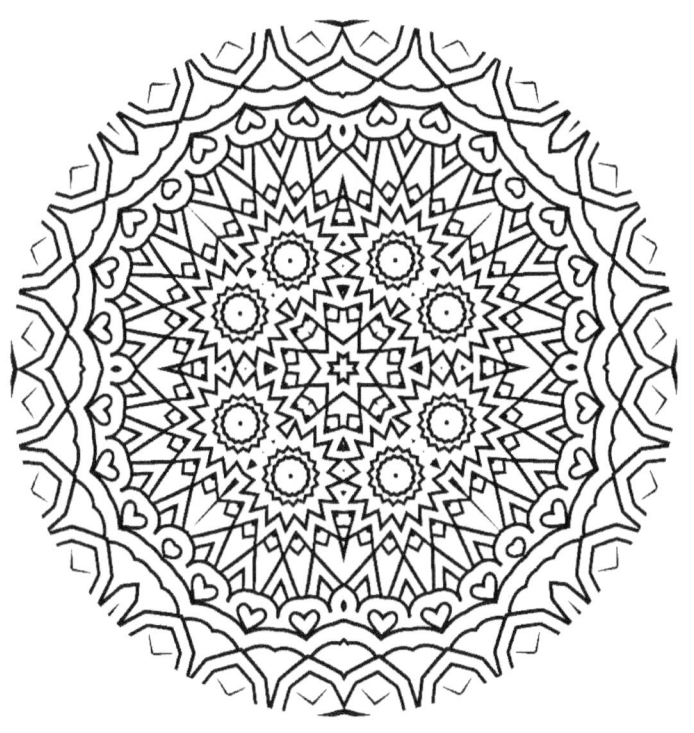

www.ingramcontent.com/pod-product-compliance
Lightning Source LLC
Chambersburg PA
CBHW070359190526
45169CB00003B/1042